UNDERSTANDING
PROGRAMMING & LOGIC

Matt Anniss

raintree

a Capstone company — publishers for children

Raintree is an imprint of Capstone Global Library Limited, a company incorporated in England and Wales having its registered office at 7 Pilgrim Street, London, EC4V 6LB – Registered company number: 6695582

www.raintree.co.uk
myorders@raintreepublishers.co.uk

Edited by Linda Staniford and Chris Harbo
Designed by Richard Parker and Tim Bond
Original illustrations © Capstone Global Library 2015
Illustrated by Nigel Dobbyn (Beehive Illustration)
Picture research by Jo Miller
Production by Victoria Fitzgerald
Originated by Capstone Global Library Ltd
Printed and bound in China by CTPS

ISBN 978 1 406 28974 9
18 17 16 15 14
10 9 8 7 6 5 4 3 2 1

British Library Cataloguing in Publication Data
A full catalogue record for this book is available from the British Library.

Acknowledgements
We would like to thank the following for permission to reproduce photographs:

Alamy: ©Bon Appetit, 8, ©Indiascapes, 12, ©Jeff Greenberg, 20; Corbis: ©Tim Pannell, 4; Dreamstime: ©Konstantin Yuganov, 34; Getty Images: Getty Images Entertainment/John M. Heller, 24, The Image Bank/B2M Productions, 36; Newscom: VWPics/Ton Koene, 42; iStockphoto: ©AvailableLight, 32, ©gchutka, 6, ©stockbart, 40; Shutterstock: Alliance, 10, Kellie L. Folkerts, 16, Anton Foltin, 30, isak55, 28, mast3r, 38, num_skyman, 26, Yurchyks, 14, supergenijalac, 18, Viktoria Kazakova, cover; Wikimedia: 22.

Design Elements: Shutterstock: HunThomas, vectorlib.com (throughout)

We would like to thank Andrew Connell for his invaluable help in the preparation of this book.

CONTENTS

Some words are shown in bold, **like this**. You can find out what they mean by looking in the glossary.

INTRODUCTION: WHAT ARE PROGRAMS?

It's hard to imagine living in a world without computer **programs**, and yet just 50 years ago they did not exist. Today, computer programs touch almost every aspect of our day-to-day lives. They're inside our computers, tablets and mobile phones, but also hidden away in every electronic **device** we use, from fridges and microwaves, to bedside alarm clocks, televisions and games consoles.

▲Computer programs now touch our lives in so many different ways.

COMPUTER FUTURE

Thanks to amazing new computer programs, it is now possible to control the lights and heating in your home by using a mobile phone or tablet computer, even if you're hundreds or thousands of miles away!

All around us

It doesn't stop there, either. Computer programs are used to help turn traffic lights on and off, make security lights switch on when you walk past, and even make street lights flicker into life at a set time every day. If something is electronic, it relies on computer programs to tell it how to operate.

Do it yourself

Although computer programs seem very complicated – and some are – many are actually surprisingly simple. Programs follow simple rules based on maths and science. You can even create your own simple programs, at home or in the classroom, if you follow the rules of logical reasoning.

THE KNOWLEDGE

Computer programs are a set of instructions that tell a device how to work. The program sets out the process the device has to go through to complete a task, and makes sure the device completes that process.

CHAPTER 1: WHAT IS LOGICAL REASONING?

Logical reasoning is a complicated term for a very simple idea. It's the process of getting something done or solving a problem by breaking it down into a series of smaller, simpler steps. This is also called decomposition.

▶If you play computer games, you will have used logical reasoning to solve puzzles and move on to the next part of the story.

Logical reasoning in daily life

We use logical reasoning a lot in our day-to-day lives, from solving difficult questions in maths lessons, to piecing together clues to advance to the next level on a computer game.

If you've been shopping, you'll also have used logical reasoning to work out how best to spend your pocket money. You might want to buy two comics and a bag of sweets, but the shop stocks 10 different comics and 20 different bags of sweets, all of which cost different amounts. By using logic, you can make a reasoned decision as to which two comics and one bag of sweets you can afford.

Day-to-day logic

The rules of logical reasoning can be applied to even the simplest of tasks, such as making a cup of hot chocolate. Using logical reasoning, you would break down the process of making hot chocolate into the following steps:

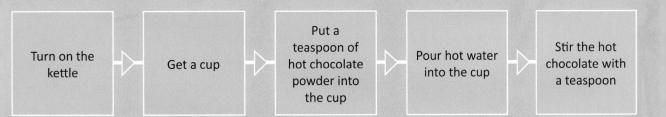

| Turn on the kettle | Get a cup | Put a teaspoon of hot chocolate powder into the cup | Pour hot water into the cup | Stir the hot chocolate with a teaspoon |

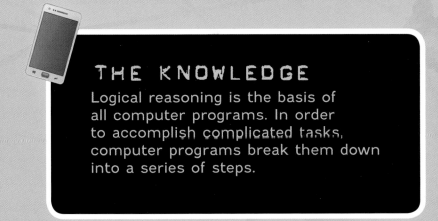

THE KNOWLEDGE

Logical reasoning is the basis of all computer programs. In order to accomplish complicated tasks, computer programs break them down into a series of steps.

◄Almost any task in our daily lives, including making lunch, can be broken down into smaller steps using logical reasoning.

Solving problems using logical reasoning

Logical reasoning can be used to work out the solution to almost any problem, regardless of the situation. If you went to your doctor complaining of a headache, runny nose and temperature, he or she would use logical reasoning to work out whether you had a cold, flu or something more serious. Similarly, a football manager would use logical reasoning to decide what tactics to use in a match, based on the strengths and weaknesses of the players in the team.

Easy process

Using logical reasoning to find the solution to a problem is simple. Identify all the possible causes of the issue and examine them one by one. Sooner or later, you'll find the root of the problem. Once you've done that, you can work out how to fix the problem.

Here's an everyday example to help make things a bit clearer. You switch on your bedside lamp and the light doesn't come on. You'd use the following logical reasoning to solve the problem.

DO'S AND DON'TS

Never try to fix broken electrical equipment. Always get an adult to check the faulty equipment for you.

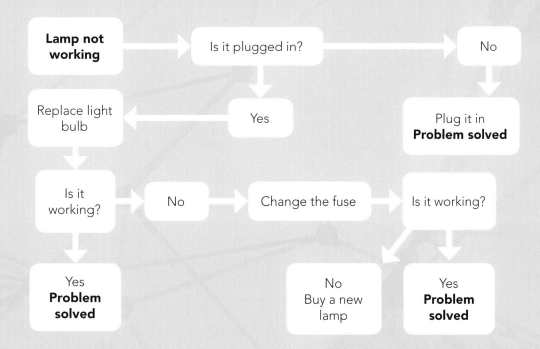

Lamp not working → Is it plugged in? → No

Is it plugged in? → Yes → Replace light bulb

No → Plug it in **Problem solved**

Replace light bulb → Is it working? → No → Change the fuse → Is it working?

Is it working? → Yes **Problem solved**

Is it working? → No Buy a new lamp

Is it working? → Yes **Problem solved**

You can do it!

Whether breaking complicated tasks into simple steps or finding the solutions to problems, logical reasoning forms the basis of all computer **programming**. If you can break down processes and problems into simple steps, as we've done above, then you can create your own computer programs.

Logic and computers

Computers rarely do things randomly, unless you ask them to. This is because they follow the rules of logical reasoning. Computer programs complete tasks in a logical way, by following a special set of instructions called an **algorithm**.

▶In the same way as you follow a set of instructions in a recipe to bake a cake or make cookies, computer programs use a set of instructions to complete a task.

THE KNOWLEDGE

An algorithm is a step-by-step list of directions that need to be followed to solve a problem. The directions must be simple enough for the computer to complete the task quickly, without confusion.

Real world algorithms

Algorithms aren't just used by computers. Any set of instructions with logical steps to follow can be considered an algorithm. If you build a model house out of plastic bricks by following step-by-step instructions, you're using an algorithm.

Computers rely on a huge number of algorithms to operate. Some of these are built into the computer, while others are user defined. This means the user (for example, yourself) tells it what to do.

Many tasks

Even fairly simple computer tasks, such as checking for emails, are actually a **sequence** of smaller algorithms completed one after the other. For example, to get an email, your computer has to send a request to another computer (known as a server) over the internet. The server computer then runs an algorithm to check if you have new messages. If you do, another algorithm sends the email to your computer, which uses another algorithm to display it on screen.

> You click the "get email" button on your email program

> Email program connects to the internet and sends request to email server to get new mail

> email server uses algorithm to check for new mail

> Email server finds new mail and sends it to your computer

> New emails appear on your computer screen

CHAPTER 2: WHAT IS COMPUTER PROGRAMMING?

◀Computer programmers write algorithms, which together form the basis of computer programs. Computer programming might seem complicated, but anyone can do it if they understand the basics!

Computer programs don't just appear out of thin air. Programs need algorithms – instructions written by experts called computer programmers. The process of creating these algorithms and programs is called computer programming.

Simple instructions

At a basic level, computer programming is simply giving computers instructions in order for them to complete a task, or a set of tasks. In computer programming, these instructions are known as **commands**. This is because you command the computer to do something, whether it's moving an object on the screen or loading a game.

Sequences

Some basic computer programs only need a single instruction, or command, to complete a task. Examples of single-command programs include the ticket barriers in car parks, and electronic doors where you press a button to open or close them.

Most programs are a bit more advanced than this, though. They need a sequence of instructions, or commands, to do something. Sequences are the basis of algorithms and almost all computer programs.

Using a lift is an easy-to-understand example of a basic sequence. It combines commands from a user, and commands built into the program that controls the lift.

  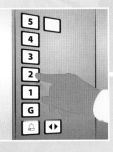 

▲Press the button to call the lift. This commands the lift to stop at your floor.

▲The lift stops at your floor and its program tells it to open the doors. You get in.

▲Press a button to tell the lift which floor you want to go to. This commands the lift to stop at that floor.

▲The lift stops at the floor you want to get off at. Its program tells it to open the doors, so that you can walk out.

13

▲When someone asks you whether you'd like a sweet, it's a straightforward choice between yes and no. Computer programs often include yes and no answers that must be answered.

Selection

In life, we often have to make simple yes or no choices. Do you want to come out and play football? Do you have enough money to buy your favourite comic? There are only two answers to these questions and it's up to you to select the right choice.

Yes or no?

Computers have to answer yes/no questions all the time (though not whether they'd like to kick a ball around). In many programs, there are questions built in. The computer must answer that question in order to move on to the next stage of the sequence. What action it takes depends on the answer. In computer programming, this is known as **selection**.

Answer the question

Let's use the example of checking for email. When you press the "get new email" button in your email program, it sends a request over the internet to the email server to retrieve any new messages. This asks the email server a question: are there any new messages? If the answer is yes, the email server will then move on to the next part of the sequence and send any new messages to your email program.

THE KNOWLEDGE

Some more complex computer programs have many selections built into them. For example, when you switch on your PC, the start-up program will ask each individual part of the computer (for example the keyboard, CD drive and monitor screen) if it's working or not.

▲The computer programs included in emergency vehicles use a repetition command to make their famous blue lights flash on and off.

Repetition

Computer programmers don't just use selection to ask questions in their programs. They also use the **repeat** command to make their programs perform a command, or set of commands, over and over again. Using the repeat instruction saves time, cuts down the amount of instructions you have to write into the program and allows you to do some quite cool things.

On and off

You could use the repeat command to make a buzzer come off and on every 10 seconds, or turn a light bulb on and off quickly, so that it flashes like the blue lights on a police car.

Repeat the sequence

If you wanted to do this, you'd write a very simple program. You'd start by creating a repeat command, telling the computer how many times you'd like it to do the sequence that follows (as an example, let's say 20). You'd then give it instructions to turn the light bulb on and then off. When you told it to start the sequence, it would then turn the lights on and off 20 times and then stop.

In programming **code**, your simple flashing lights sequence would look like this:

```
Repeat 20
[turn light on
turn light off]
```

Did you know?

In computer programming, you're in charge. If you want your light to flash more slowly, you can add in a **"delay"** command. This tells the program how long you want it to wait before moving on to the next stage in the sequence.

Procedures

Creating a computer program can be a long, slow process. Helpfully, there are short cuts designed to save time and make your life easier. For example, you can teach a computer to do something using **procedures**.

◄ Programmers use procedures - also called subprograms or **subroutines** - in programs to simplify the programming process, making complicated tasks, such as telling a machine how to paint a car, so much easier.

THE KNOWLEDGE

Procedures are frequently used sequences of commands that can be saved and given a title. This means that instead of writing out loads of commands over and over again, you can just type in a single word and the computer will do something amazing!

Make your own procedures

If you wanted to create a computer program that made a light bulb flash and then an alarm ring, you would create two separate sequences and then save them as procedures. The flashing lights procedure might be called "lights 1" and the alarm procedure could be titled "alarm 1".

The commands in each procedure would look like this (see illustration below). The "repeat 20" command tells the program to turn the lights on and off 20 times, while the "delay 20" command tells the program to wait 20 seconds before turning the alarm off.

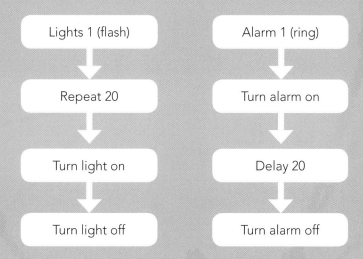

Once you've created these sequences and saved them as procedures, you can trigger them by including their names in the program, like this:

Lights 1 (flash)
Alarm 1 (ring)

Over and over again

Programmers use procedures all the time. Most large computer programs are made up of lots of procedures strung together. Once a procedure has been created, it can be used time and time again.

CHAPTER 3: WHAT CAN I DO WITH COMPUTER PROGRAMMING?

▲Computer programming is at the centre of all of the electronic gadgets we take for granted today.

It's no use knowing the basic concepts behind computer programming, if you don't know what to do with them. It would be like knowing the rules of basketball without being able to pass or shoot, or understanding how to make your own clothes without knowing how to get dressed in the morning!

Programming for life

Fortunately, computer programming is really useful, and there are loads of cool things we can use programming to do. Computer programming is at the heart of all modern electronic devices, from telephones, televisions and tablets, to DVD players, games consoles and computers. Some of the programs that help these devices work are relatively simple, while others are hugely complicated. They all have one thing in common, though: someone created the program that allows them to do amazing things.

Did you know?

The world's first computer programmer was a British woman called Ada Lovelace. In 1842, she wrote an algorithm that could be used to work out basic sums on Charles Babbage's Difference Engine, now considered to be the world's first mechanical computer.

What about me?

Even if you're a genius, it's highly unlikely that you'd be able to create a computer program to run a DVD player, or design your own game from the beginning – not yet, at least! However, there are lots of things you can do with basic programming knowledge, either at home or at school.

With a few exceptions, most computer programs help you do one of three things: solve problems, make choices or control things.

▲The Jacquard Loom, invented in 1801 to help weave complicated patterns into cloth, was one of the first machines to use programming as we know it today.

Solving problems

Problem solving has always been the number one use of programming. Even before modern electronic computers were invented, people were designing programmable machines to solve complicated problems.

Did you know?

The first programmable machine wasn't a computer, but rather the Jacquard Loom – a machine that could weave different patterns into clothing by reading a series of cards with holes punched into them.

Still solving problems

Solving problems is the basis of all modern computing, even the simple gadgets you use at school. Calculators are designed to solve the problem of adding, subtracting, multiplying and dividing numbers.

When you tap numbers into your calculator during maths lessons, you are in effect programming it. You have programmed it to do the maths for you. It can do this because the makers of the calculator put an algorithm inside it capable of finding correct answers to hard sums.

Program your own calculations

Computer programs called **spreadsheets** allow you to solve many maths-related problems. Spreadsheets look like big tables, with loads of columns and rows. The boxes inside the tables are called **cells**.

Spreadsheets are great because you have total control over them. You can tell them to add, subtract or multiply numbers contained in certain cells, by creating a **formula**. This is the calculation you'd like it to do for you.

This might sound complicated, but it isn't. Here's an example of a basic spreadsheet you might use to work out the cost of things you'd like to buy.

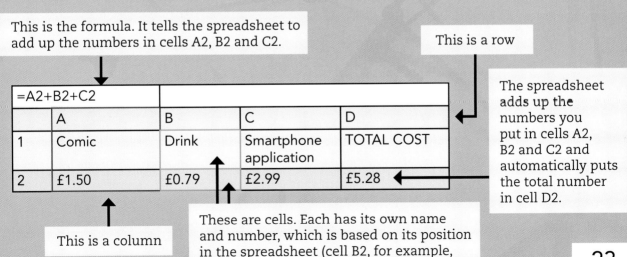

This is the formula. It tells the spreadsheet to add up the numbers in cells A2, B2 and C2.

This is a row

The spreadsheet adds up the numbers you put in cells A2, B2 and C2 and automatically puts the total number in cell D2.

=A2+B2+C2			
	A	B	C	D
1	Comic	Drink	Smartphone application	TOTAL COST
2	£1.50	£0.79	£2.99	£5.28

This is a column

These are cells. Each has its own name and number, which is based on its position in the spreadsheet (cell B2, for example, means the cell in column B, row 2).

23

Making choices

Programming isn't just useful for solving problems. It can also be used to help us make choices, and learn the effect our choices have on something. Computer programs where we have to make choices that affect what happens next are called **simulations**.

▲Formula 1 drivers use driving simulators like this one to help learn the layout of race tracks and fine tune their skills.

Useful simulations

Computer simulations can be very useful. Before being allowed to fly a plane, pilots train for a long period of time on a flight simulator. It feels like they're flying a plane, but they're just plugged into a computer that's been programmed to react to their actions. Simulators are safe and allow people to learn from their mistakes without putting themselves in danger.

Choices and outcomes

The choices we make in simulations affect what happens next, just like our choices in real life. If you watered a plant every day, it would grow tall. If you rarely water it, it won't. If you play a driving game, go too fast and lose control, you'll crash and your race would be over. If you keep control, you might win the race.

You can find out just exactly what difference your choices make in a simulator by noting down the results of every choice. If you do something once and something happens, it's almost certain to happen again if you do it next time. Using programming, we can make programs that simulate almost any situation.

Controlling things

One of the coolest things you can do with computer programming is controlling things. Algorithms designed to control things are known as control sequences. The punch card system used to make the Jacquard Loom weave patterns on cloth was an early example of a control sequence.

You're in charge

Control sequences are all around us. When you press play on your MP3 player to listen to a song, the control sequence kicks in, turning the information stored in the MP3 file into music you can hear.

▶The automatic barriers in car parks are a good example of a control sequence. They're programmed to lift up when a car stops in front of them.

COMPUTER FUTURE

In 2013, Google unveiled a pair of glasses that allows you to do loads of cool things, just by speaking basic commands. Each command triggers a different control sequence. So, if you say "OK glasses, take a video" the camera attached to the glasses will turn itself on and start recording. Amazing!

Open and shut

Another great example of a control sequence is the one that makes automatic doors work. These appear to open by magic when we walk up to them. In fact, their control sequence is programmed to open the doors when somebody walks onto a pressure pad hidden underneath the floor in front of them, or passes close to a motion-sensitive camera positioned above the doors.

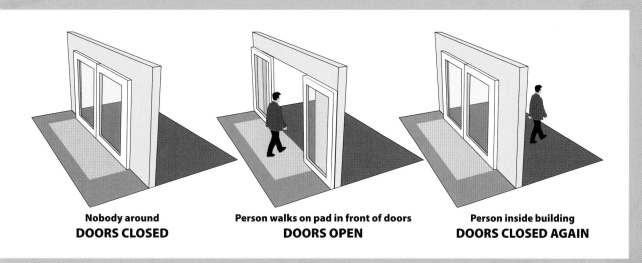

Nobody around
DOORS CLOSED

Person walks on pad in front of doors
DOORS OPEN

Person inside building
DOORS CLOSED AGAIN

Speak the right language

It's easy to create basic algorithms to control devices such as lights, buzzers and even doors. If you want to try this for yourself, you'll need to understand what **programming languages** are, and how they're used.

CHAPTER 4: HOW DO I USE PROGRAMMING LANGUAGES?

Programming languages are used to give instructions to a computer, or electronic gadget, in a form that it understands.

◀Programming languages seem complicated, but they're actually designed to make it simpler to give computers instructions.

THE KNOWLEDGE

Programming languages are the basis of computer programs. Without them, there would be no programs at all. Every programming language is made up of a set of commands, each of which is designed to make the computer perform a different task.

Different languages

There are thousands of programming languages. Each is designed for a specific purpose and is capable of doing different things. For example, the programming language used to create software **applications** (what we call apps) for Apple smartphones and tablets is Objective-C, while the language traditionally used to create websites is called HTML (short for Hypertext Markup Language).

Each programming language has its own set of commands, which programmers must learn if they're going to write a program in that language.

Simple things

Thankfully, most programming languages are very simple. They use easy-to-understand commands, such as "start", "repeat" (do something again), "delay" (wait for a period of time) and "stop". They feature simple instructions that both you and the computer can follow. So, if you want it to ring a bell very loudly, it will do just that.

Did you know?

Instructions to a computer written in a programming language are known as code. If you string a sequence of commands together (for example: start, turn light on, delay, stop), then you've written some code.

▲Pushing down a plunger to set off an explosion that demolishes a building is a great example of a control sequence at work. The plunger is the input device, and the dynamite inside the building is the output device.

Input and output devices

You now understand the importance of programming languages and are probably itching to try them out for yourself! Before you can start controlling devices using your computer and some basic programming, you need to understand the difference between **input devices** and **output devices**, and how they're used.

THE KNOWLEDGE

Input devices are things like switches, buttons and levers. Outputs are signals to devices such as lights, buzzers and motors. Input devices send signals to the processor, which uses programs to process the data and then may send a signal to the output device.

Get set up

To create your own control sequences, you'll need some input devices, output devices, and a control box to plug them into. The control box is then plugged into your computer. Once you've done that, you're ready to start programming.

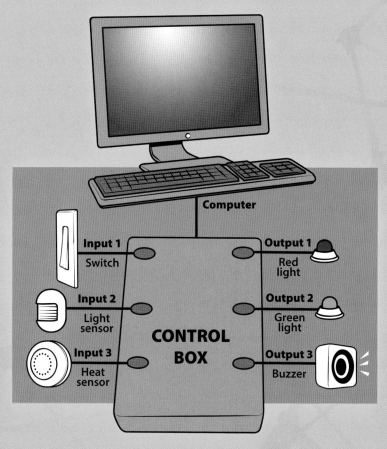

You're in control

When everything's plugged in, you can use your computer to control a number of different variables. A variable is simply anything that can be changed and controlled. In this example, the inputs and outputs are the variables. These variables can be programmed to do things.

With all of these input and output signals, there are loads of things you can do. By simply typing instructions into a program, you can flick the switch to make lights flash, turn a buzzer on or even create your own miniature light show!

▲Security lights turn themselves on when it gets dark. This is because they've been programmed to only come on if certain environmental conditions are met.

Basic controls

Programming languages are easy to learn, because most of the commands are really simple. Once you've memorized them, you'll be writing programs in no time at all. Remember: programs are just step-by-step instructions for the computer to follow.

Get with the program

Here's an example of a basic sequence of commands that we want the computer to follow. We want it to turn on a light (output 1) and make it flash when someone flicks a switch (input 1). It contains selection (the sequence only starts when somebody flicks the switch) and could be saved as a procedure (for example, as 'flash 1').

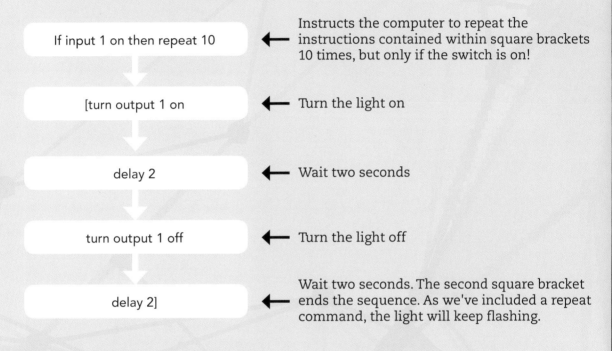

If input 1 on then repeat 10	← Instructs the computer to repeat the instructions contained within square brackets 10 times, but only if the switch is on!
[turn output 1 on	← Turn the light on
delay 2	← Wait two seconds
turn output 1 off	← Turn the light off
delay 2]	← Wait two seconds. The second square bracket ends the sequence. As we've included a repeat command, the light will keep flashing.

Super sensors

That's all pretty straightforward, right? You can spice things up by using different types of inputs, such as **sensors**. These are devices that respond to environmental factors, such as how hot or cold it is, or whether it is light or dark outside.

THE KNOWLEDGE

Heat sensors are used to turn on output devices, such as heaters or fans, when the temperature gets above or below a certain level. Light sensors are used to turn on outside lights when it gets dark.

33

▲When you open the fridge door, two things happen: the light comes on, and the heat sensor checks the temperature to make sure the fridge is cold enough. This is an example of a program controlling two output devices.

Controlling more than one output device

Once you've got the hang of control languages, you don't have to stop at simply controlling one output device. You can very easily use your newfound programming skills to control a number of different output devices at the same time.

Let's get serious

The more outputs you want to control, the more complicated your program will be. Instead of a few lines of commands, you'll need to be writing blocks of code. Don't worry, though – as long as you plan out your program carefully before you start, it's just a matter of stringing all those commands together in the right order.

Ring the alarm

Here's an example of how you might draw out a sequence to alternate between a light and a buzzer, using a heat sensor (input 1). The output devices will only come on when the temperature hits a certain level.

Sub-routines

This illustration is a great example of a procedure, sometimes called a sub-routine. Creating named procedures makes it much easier to write longer programs. Once a computer has been 'taught' a procedure, it remembers it. That means you can simply write the name of the procedure into your program and it will do it!

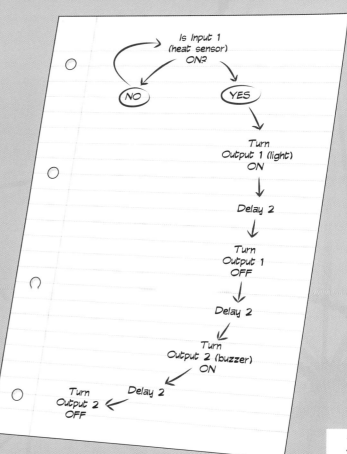

Is Input 1
(heat sensor)
ON?

NO   YES

Turn
Output 1 (light)
ON

Delay 2

Turn
Output 1
OFF

Delay 2

Turn
Output 2 (buzzer)
ON

Turn   Delay 2
Output 2
OFF

CHAPTER 5: WHAT IF MY PROGRAMMING DOESN'T WORK?

▲It's easy to get stressed if your programs don't work correctly. Thankfully, finding and correcting problems is simply a matter of double-checking your sequences and procedures.

Computer programs are great, because they do exactly what you tell them to do. If you write a program to run a motor that turns a wheel, you'd expect the wheel to start spinning. If it doesn't, it's hugely frustrating. You might want to start shouting or waving your arms, convinced that the computer is doing something strange. That's not what you told it to do, after all! Problems with programs are annoying, but also surprisingly common. So why do they happen?

Faulty instructions

Computer programs are not like you and me. We can be asked to do something, and decide how we want to do it. Computers can't do this – they only do what they're told. Computers follow the instructions laid out in their programs, working through each command in sequence until they've reached the end. This means that if your program doesn't work, there's something wrong with your instructions. Somehow, you've made a mistake.

THE KNOWLEDGE

Mistakes are common in programming. Even the best programmers in the world make mistakes. They call these mistakes errors or bugs. If a program doesn't work, it's a sign of errors.

Errors

If you're going to get into computer programming, you need to know how to spot errors. Once you know where to look, fixing problems caused by errors is surprisingly easy.

◄Finding errors can be a slow and confusing process, unless you know what you're looking for.

Did you know?

There are three main types of errors in programming.

Compilation errors: these stop your program from starting. They're usually caused by mistakes when typing code, such as spelling commands incorrectly.

Run-time errors: bugs that occur while your program is running. Usually caused by mistyped commands, or instructions that are simply impossible for the computer to carry out.

Logic errors: these are bugs that prevent your program from doing what you intended it to do. They're usually a result of writing commands in the wrong order.

Finding errors

Spotting errors is simply a matter of working through your program, step-by-step, until you find the mistake. You can then correct it and try again. More often than not, this will solve the problem.

Can you spot the errors?

We've written a program to turn a light (output 1) on and off, but it's not working. Can you find the errors?

Start

repreat 10

[turn output 1 on

delay 2

turn output 1 off

delay 2

Did you spot our three errors? The first is the misspelling of the word "repeat", which means that the computer doesn't understand the command. The second is the missing square bracket ("]"), which means the sequence to be repeated is incomplete. Finally, we've forgotten to write a "stop" command at the end of the program. If we fixed the other errors, but not that one, the light would keep flashing forever!

▲ If you make a mistake when writing with pencil, you can rub it out and change it. You can do exactly the same with errors in your programs.

How to avoid errors

As we've seen, spotting errors is easy if you know where to look. It's simply a matter of closely looking at your code, finding the mistake and then changing it. Really, it's just like deleting a word in a **word processor** and replacing it with another one.

Do it right

It's good to know you can change your programs if there's a problem, but it's even better to avoid making errors in the first place. If you get it right first time, it saves time locating and fixing the problem.

The best way to avoid errors is to be organized. That means taking time to plan your program before you start writing it, being careful when typing out commands, and then double-checking your sequences before you test them out. Drawing flow charts of the sequences, mapping out the input and output devices (that's drawing a diagram of where everything is plugged in to) and slowly reading through the code are all great ways of avoiding errors.

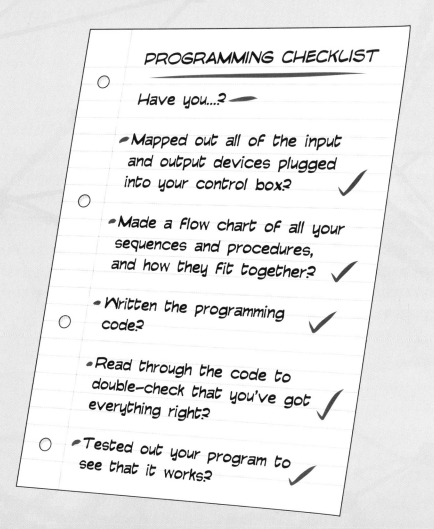

PROGRAMMING CHECKLIST

Have you....?

○ Mapped out all of the input and output devices plugged into your control box? ✓

○ Made a flow chart of all your sequences and procedures, and how they fit together? ✓

○ Written the programming code? ✓

○ Read through the code to double-check that you've got everything right? ✓

○ Tested out your program to see that it works? ✓

CONCLUSION: YOU'RE IN COMMAND!

By now, you should have got a taste for computer programming and are itching to do more. That's the great thing about programming – however confusing it might seem at first, once you know the basics it's really addictive.

▶ There's no end to where programming can lead. In future, you could be writing programs for your very own robot to perform!

COMPUTER FUTURE

One of the biggest tasks facing programmers is creating electronic devices with artificial intelligence, or the ability to think for themselves. This is only possible if programmers write hugely complicated programs that tell the devices how to respond to every possible situation. Robots capable of responding to a number of different commands do exist, but true artificial intelligence is still some way off.

The golden rules

As we've pointed out, all programming languages work to the same basic principles. Computers only understand logical reasoning, so it's just a matter of learning the commands and how you can use them to do really cool things. Once you know how to write a program in one language, you can easily learn other languages. It's like that in real life, too – once you can speak Spanish, it's easier to learn Portuguese.

Endless opportunities

Because so many electronic devices rely on programming, there are so many different things you can do with programming skills. You could create your own sound and light shows, write your own computer games, and even design a program that turns on a fan when your bedroom gets too hot. Let your imagination flow and see what you can come up with!

GLOSSARY

algorithm set of instructions with logical steps, for example a recipe, the booklet of instructions for making a model out of plastic bricks, or a computer program

application in computing, another name for a program. Applications (or apps), as you'd get on smartphones and tablet computers, are programs designed to let you do something specific (play a game, draw a picture, take a photograph).

cell term used to describe a box in a spreadsheet table

code in programming, a series of commands grouped together. An individual instruction is a command.

command instruction to a computer to do something

delay put off to a later time. In programming, the delay command means 'wait'.

device thing made for a particular purpose, for example a light bulb, an electronic calculator, or a fridge

fantasies dreams, or things created using your imagination not based on real life events. Adventure games are fantasies.

formula calculation in a spreadsheet

input device something that sends information to the computer or electrical circuit, for example a button, switch, lever or sensor

output device something that performs a task following instructions from a computer or input device, for example a light, buzzer, alarm or motor

procedure sequence of commands that can be triggered by typing the name of the procedure into a computer program

program application on a computer designed to help you carry out a specific task, or a set of tasks

programming process of writing a computer program

programming language set of rules and commands used for writing programs. There are many different programming languages around, each with their own rules and commands

repeat do something again. In programming, the 'repeat' command makes the computer repeat the following action (turning something on or off, etc).

selection computing term for an either/or question. The computer must answer the question before moving on to the next part of the program.

sensor piece of electronic equipment designed to detect changes in the world around it, for example rises or falls in temperature, or how light or dark it is outside

sequence connected series of things, usually in a logical order. For example, a sentence is a sequence of words in a logical order. In computer programming, a sequence is a series of instructions in the form of commands.

simulation computer program that allows you to pretend you're in a situation. Simulations are things like driving games and flight simulators. Simulations allow you to make choices, in order to see what difference those choices make.

spreadsheet type of computer program designed to help you keep track of numbers and do complicated sums

sub-routine another name for procedure

word processor application that allows you to write on a computer. Microsoft Word is an example of a word processor.

Books

Hello World! Computer Programming for Kids & Other Beginners Warren & Carter Sande (2nd Edition; Manning Publishing, 2013)

The History of the Computer Elizabeth Raum (Heinemann Library, 2007)

Oxford Illustrated Computer Dictionary Ian Dicks (Oxford University Press, 2009)

Video Game Programming for Kids Jonathan S. Harbour (Delmar Cengage Learning , 2012)

Websites

www.codecademy.com

This is a brilliant online resource that teaches you the basics of coding in a number of different programming languages. Simply follow the instructions on the website. It shows you how to make cool things like killer games and applications.

www.codeclub.org.uk

If you're keen to learn how to program, these people may be able to help. They run after-school programming clubs in over 600 schools around the UK. There might even be a code club at your school!

https://goggles.webmaker.org/en-US

If you've ever wondered how programmers write websites, you should visit this site. It allows you to visit web pages, see the code, and change it. You can create your own "remixes" of popular websites, such as Google and the New York Times.

www.kidsruby.com

KidsRuby is a free program that helps you learn how to write code. Follow the instructions, write your own code and see the results unfold before your eyes! It even allows you to design your own cool smartphone applications.

http://scratch.mit.edu

This great online programming course lets you program your own games, stories and animations, which you can then share with your friends. Why not try it out for yourself?

Places to visit

The National Museum of Computing
Block H, Bletchley Park, Milton Keynes, UK
www.tnmoc.org

Learn about the history of computers and programming at Britain's national museum of computing, based at Bletchley Park. During the Second World War, this was home to Colossus, one of the most important computers ever built. You can see a rebuilt version of Colossus, and see how its punch-card system worked.

The Science Museum
Exhibition Road, South Kensington, London, UK
www.sciencemuseum.org.uk

Check out the Science Museum's permanent exhibition about the history of computers. It features working versions of some of the oldest computers in the world, as well as a recreation of Charles Babbage's amazing Difference Engine – now thought of as the world's first mechanical computer.

INDEX